Austin Van Allen

Vibrant Creations

Coloring Book. Vol. 1: Flowers
A.j.v._art studios

A different kind of coloring book.

Follow on Instagram @a.j.v._art
www.ajvart.com

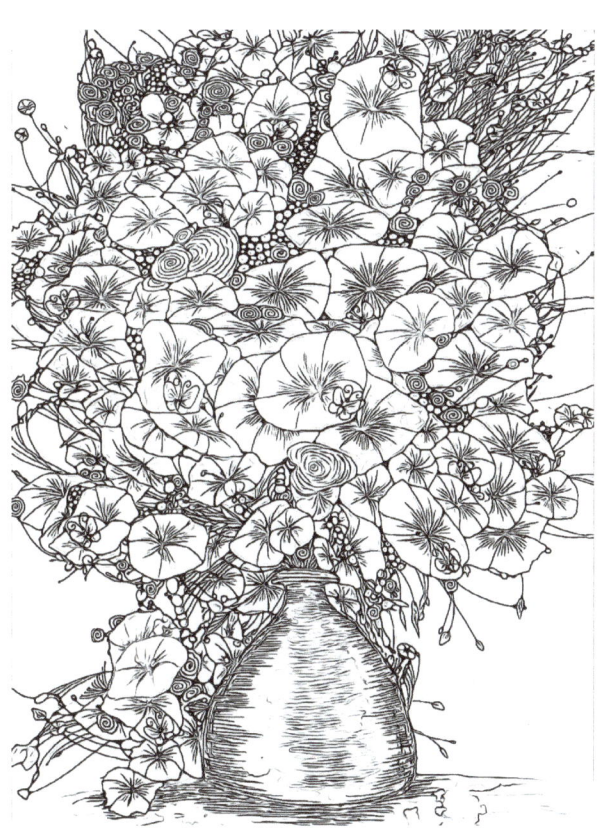

This Coloring Book Belongs to:

_____

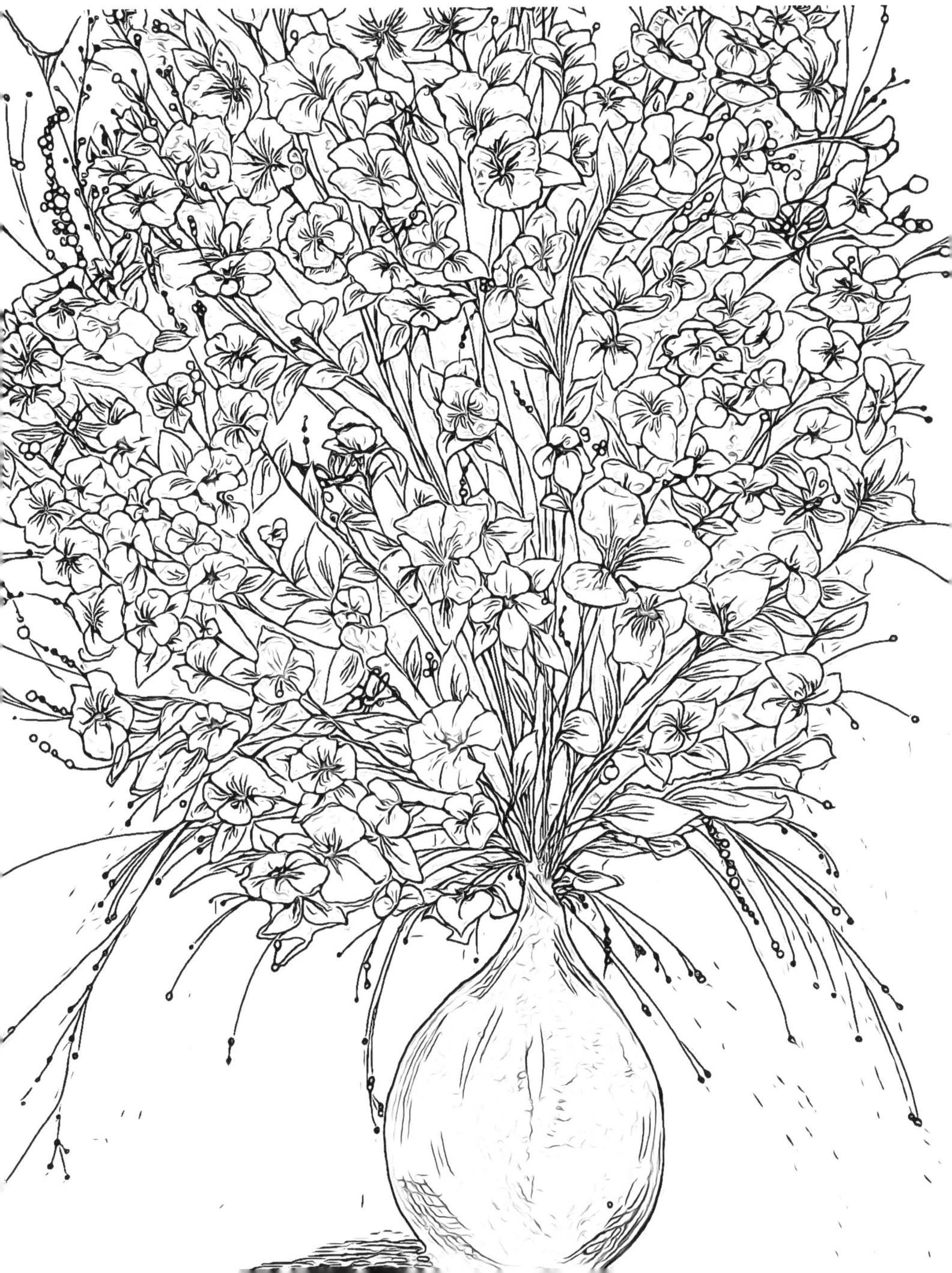

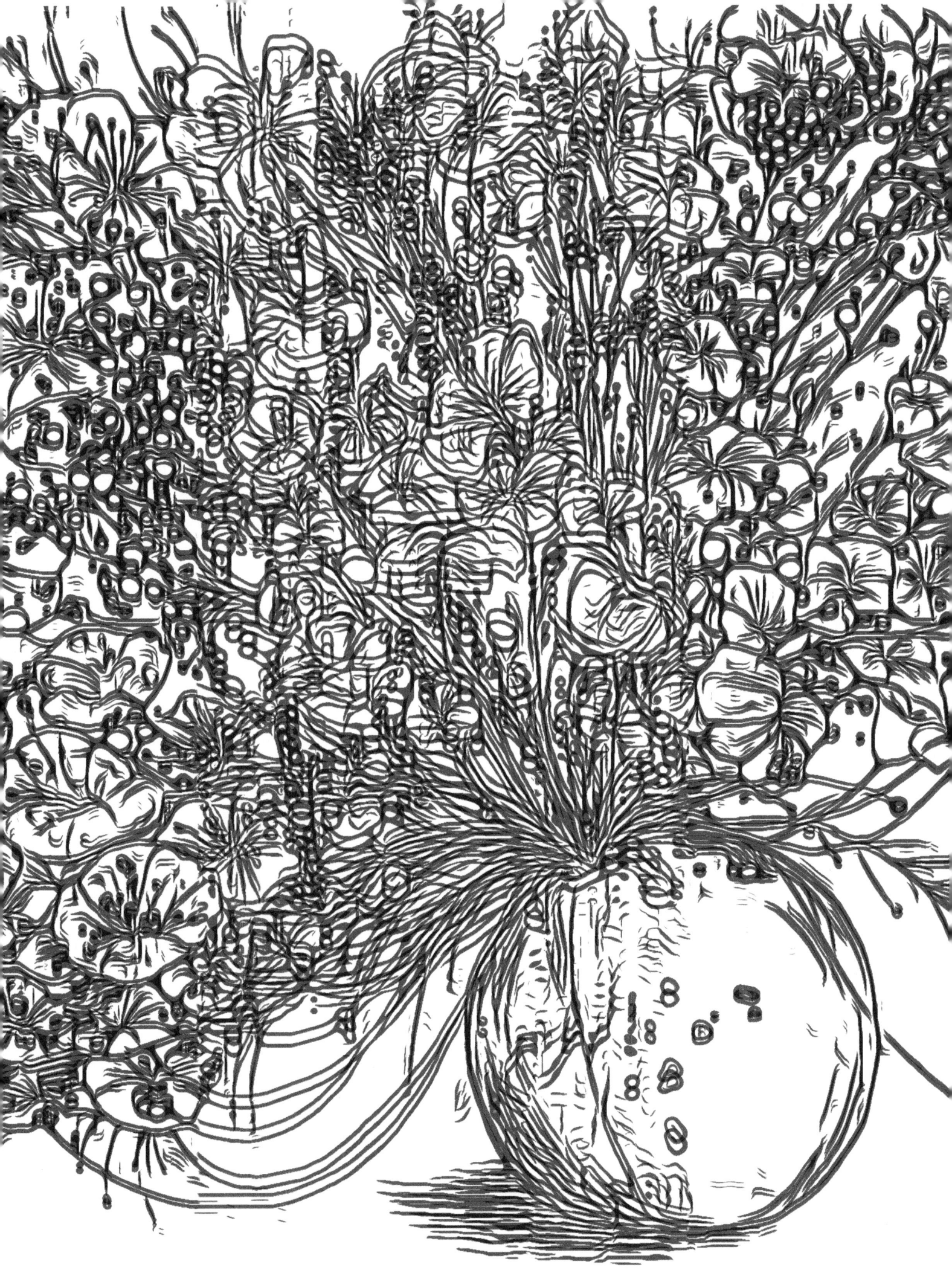

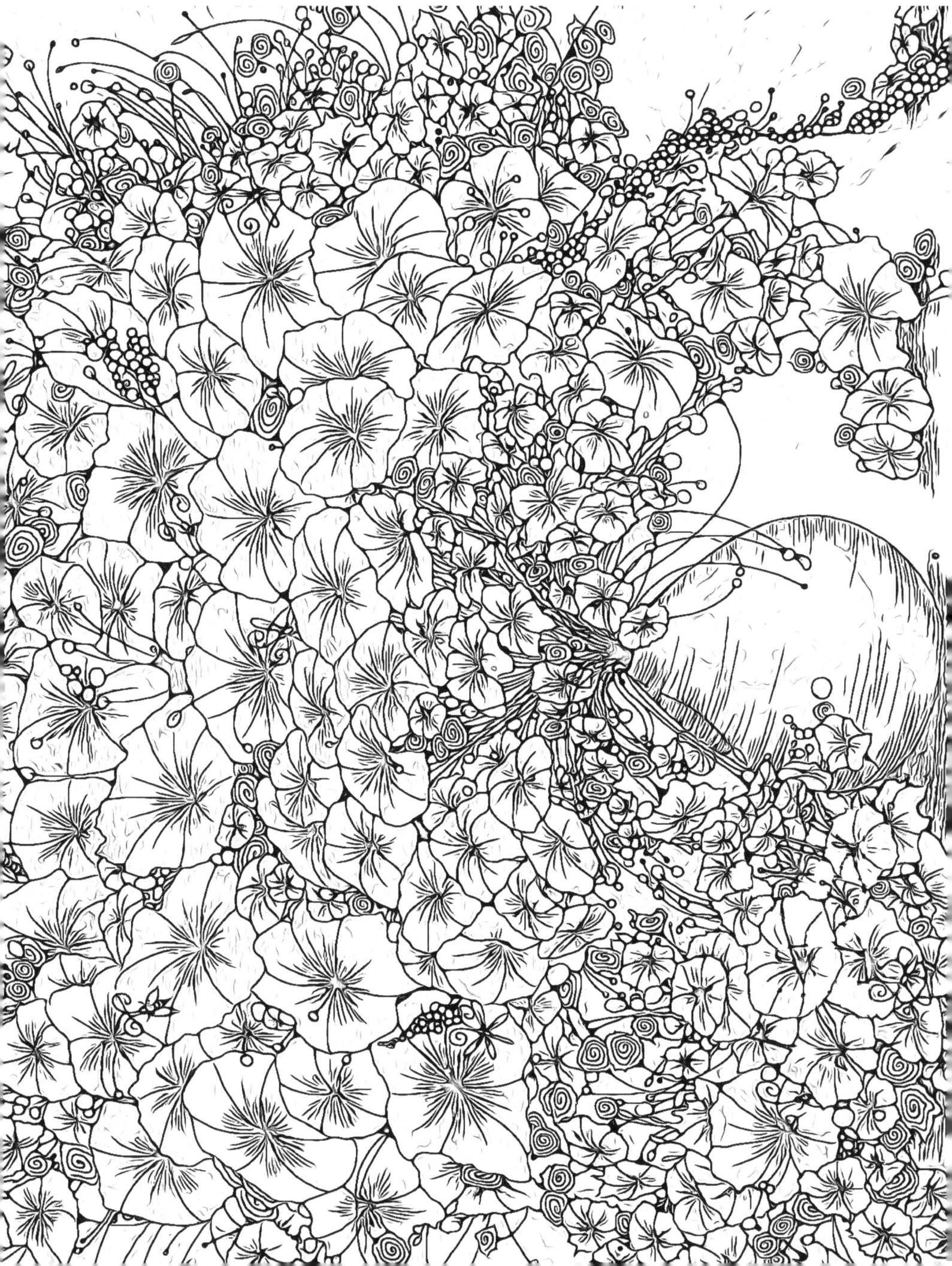

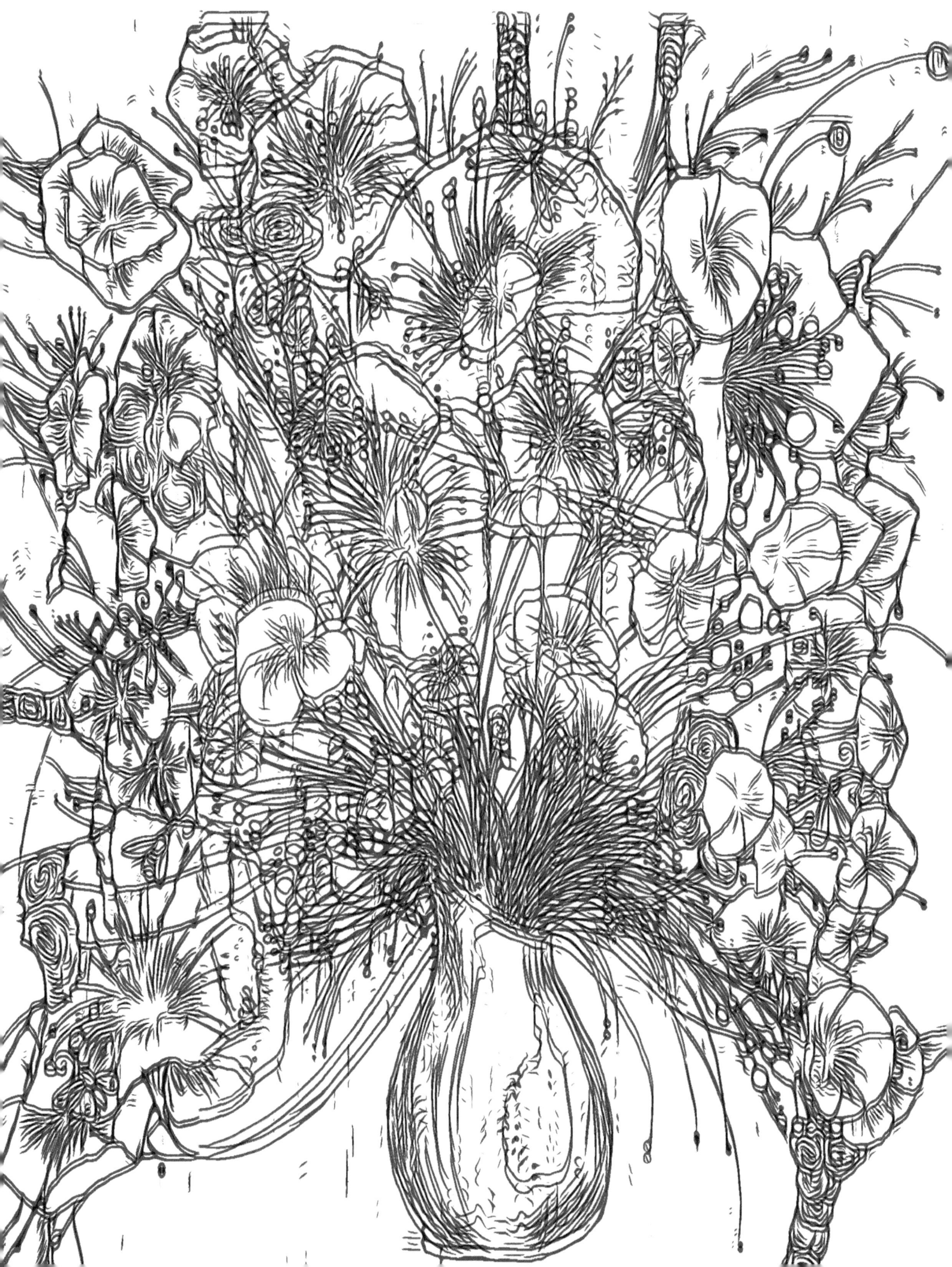

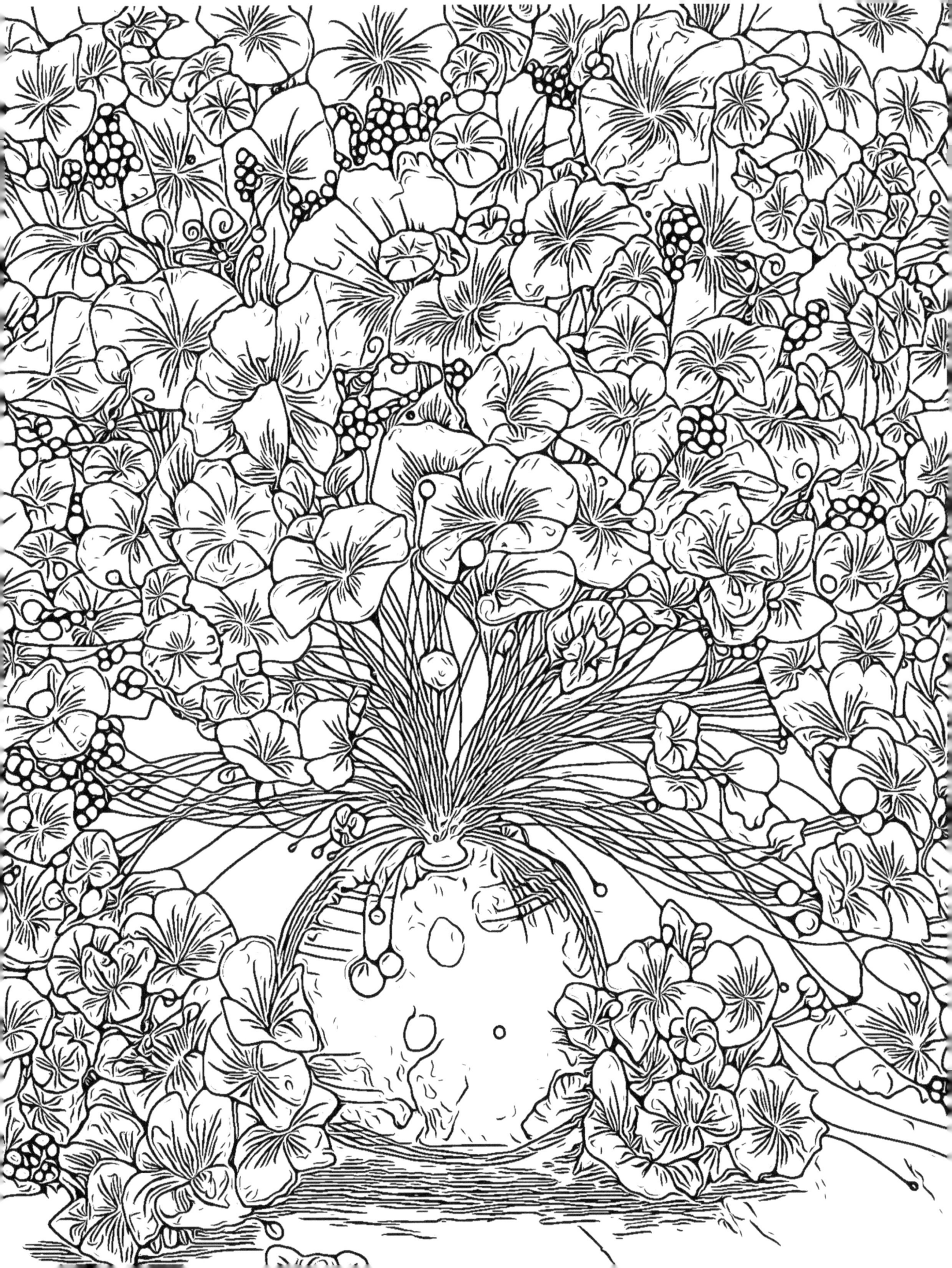

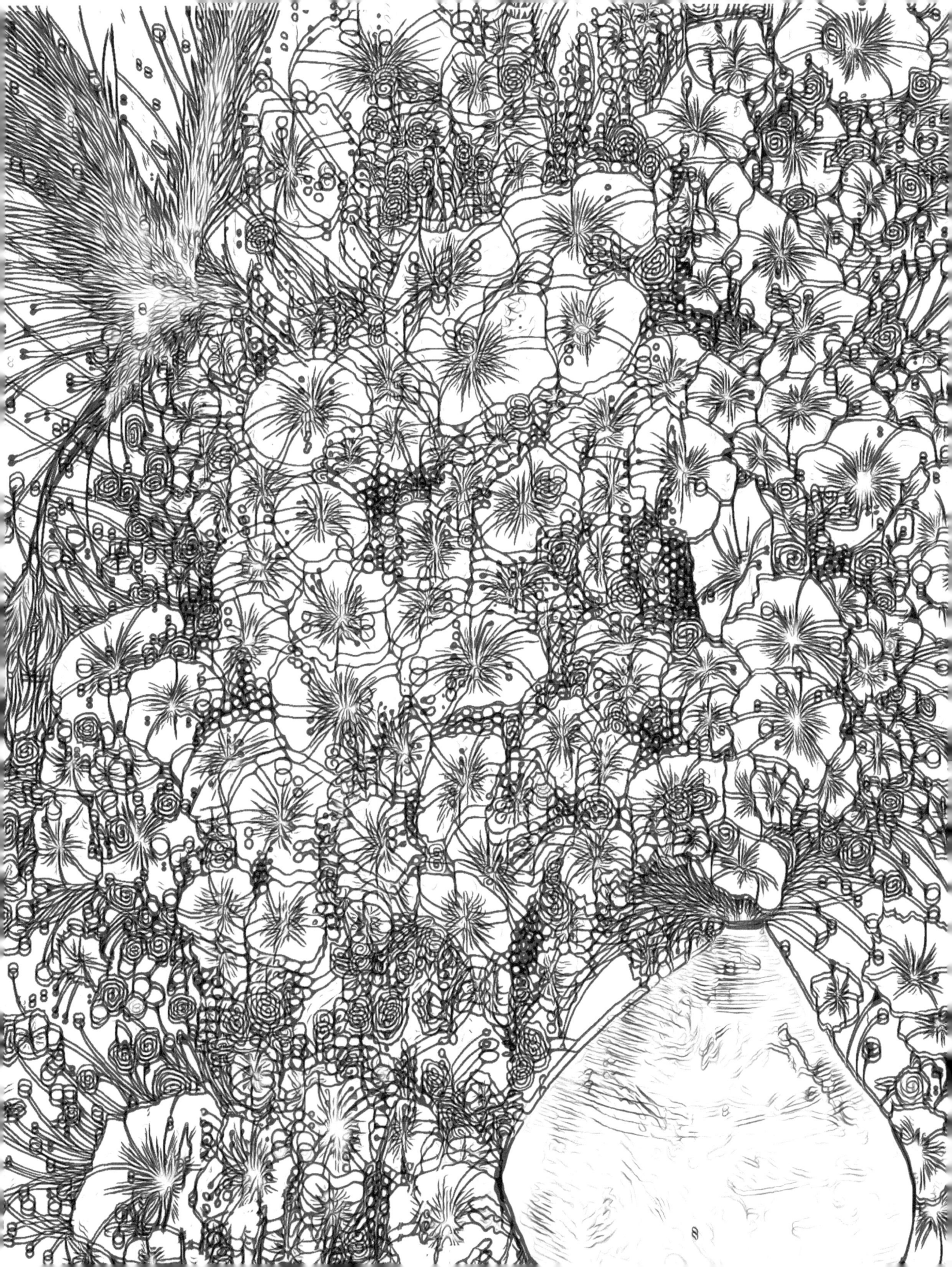

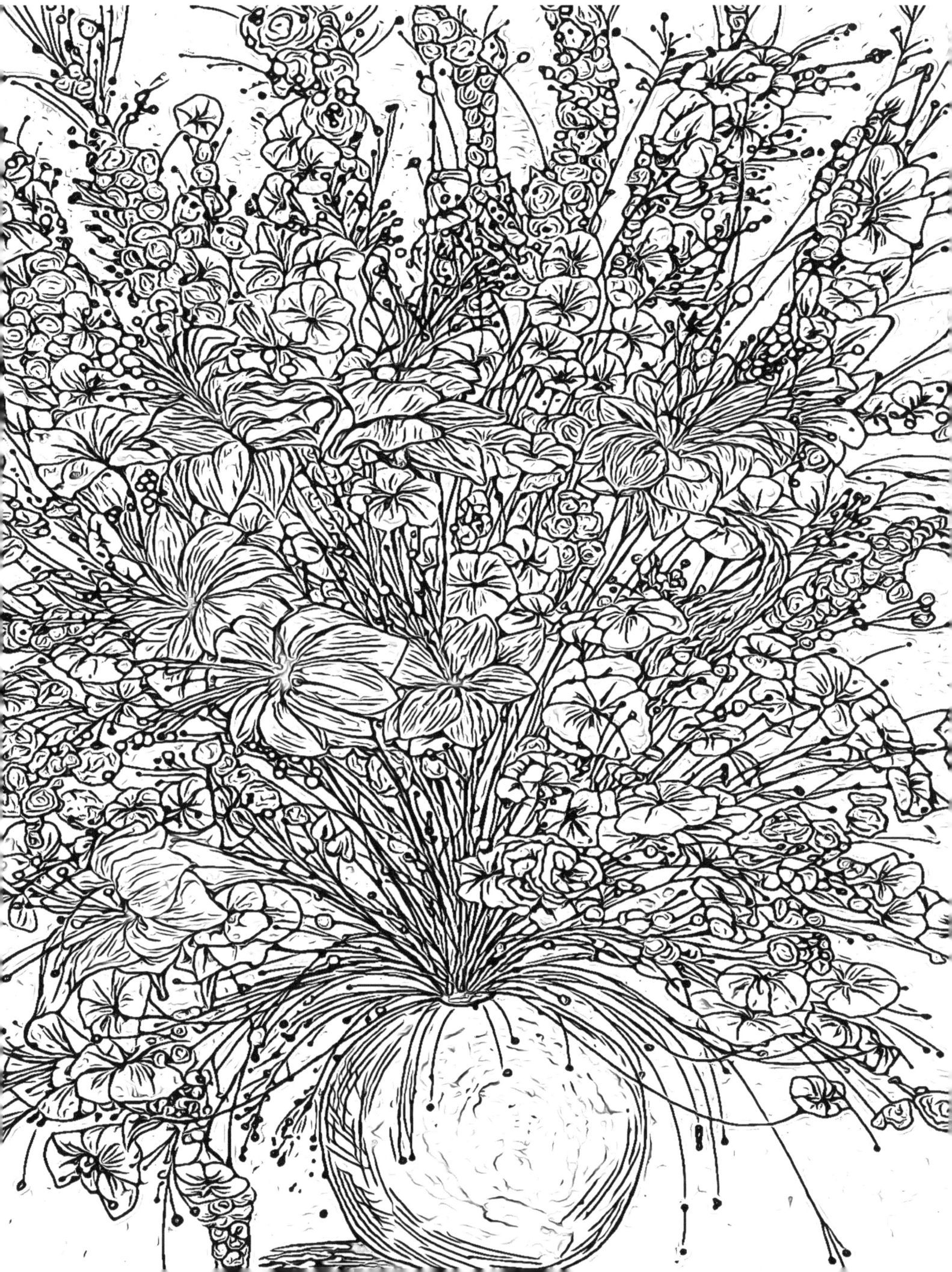

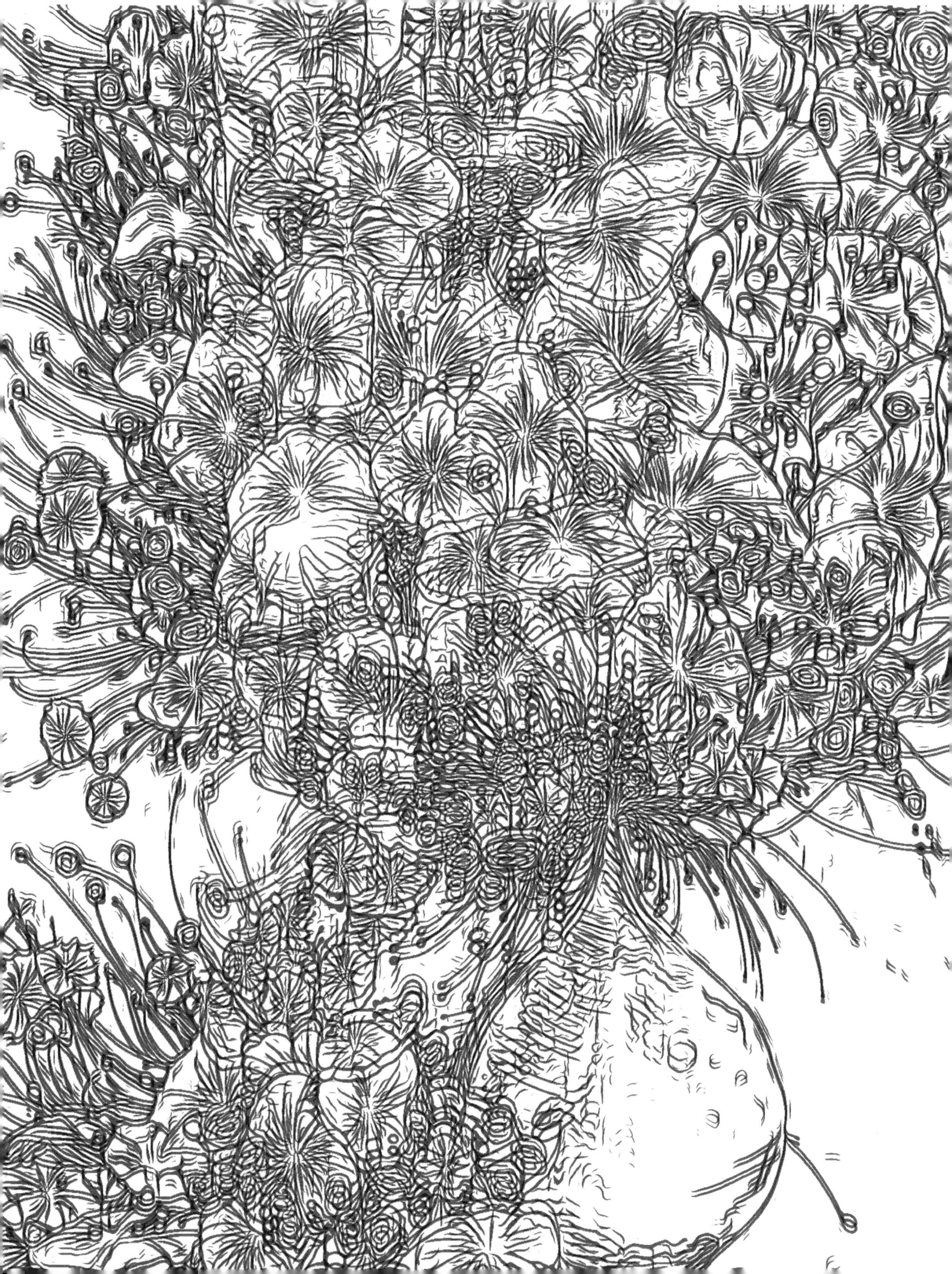

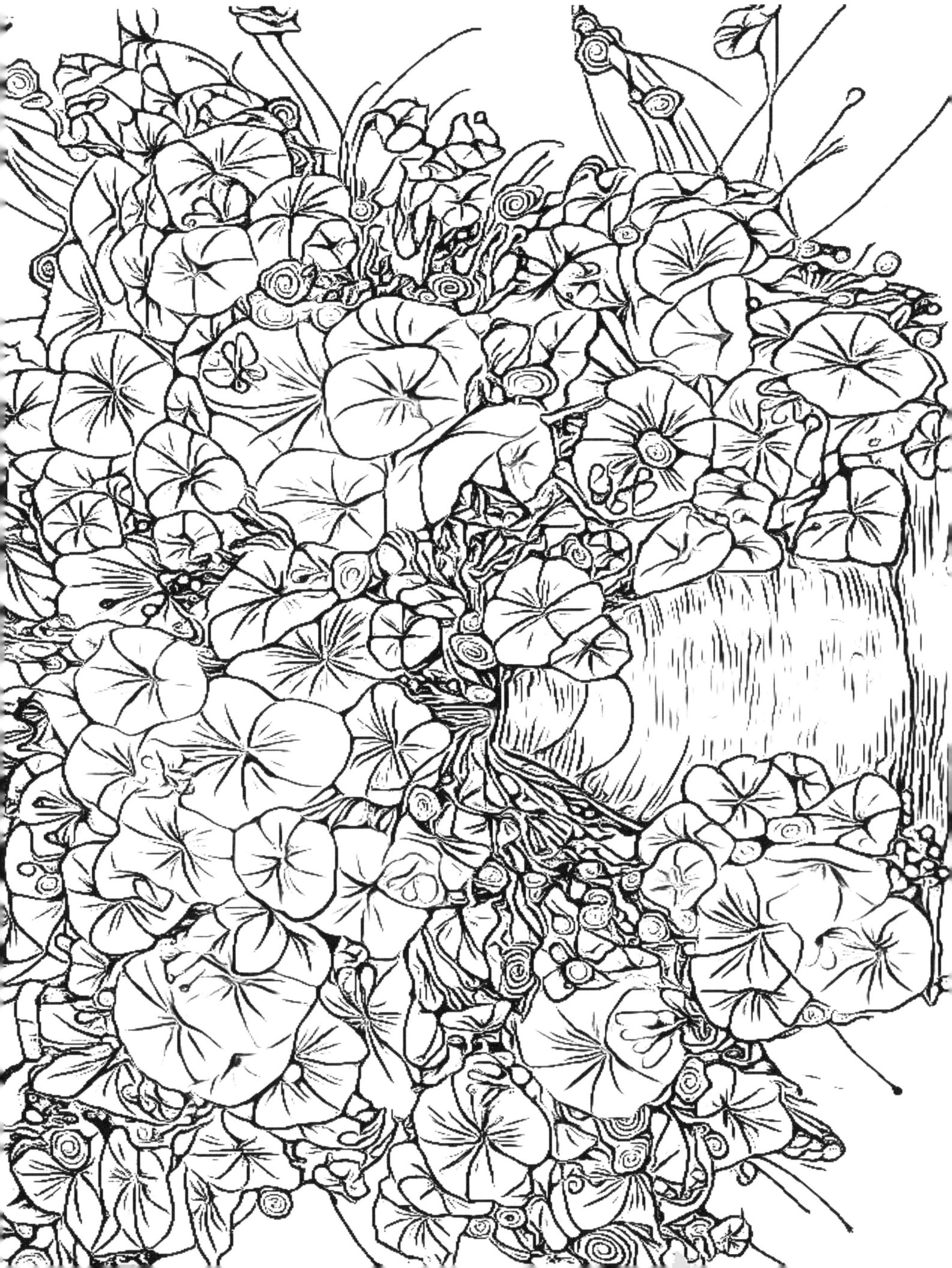

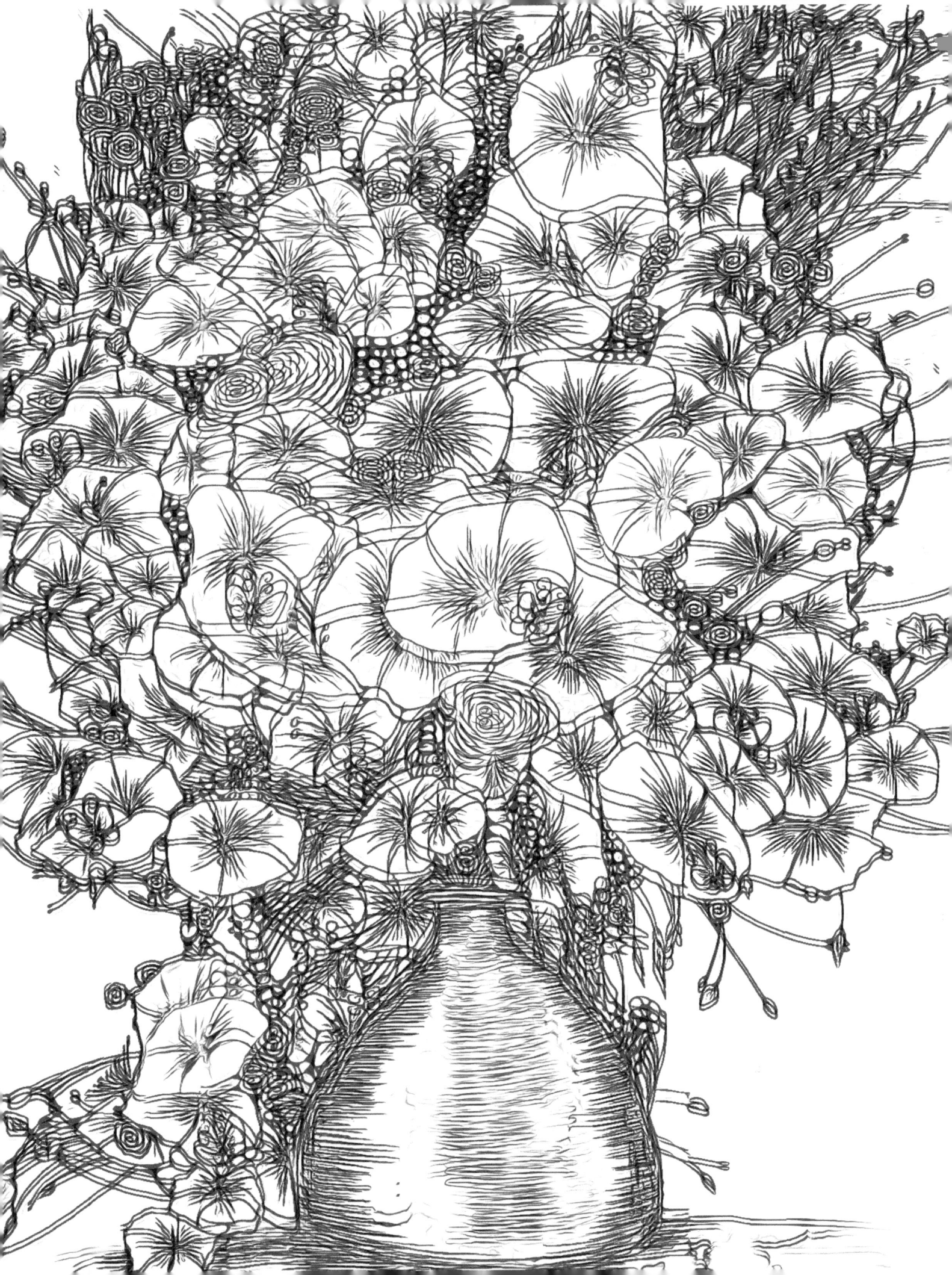

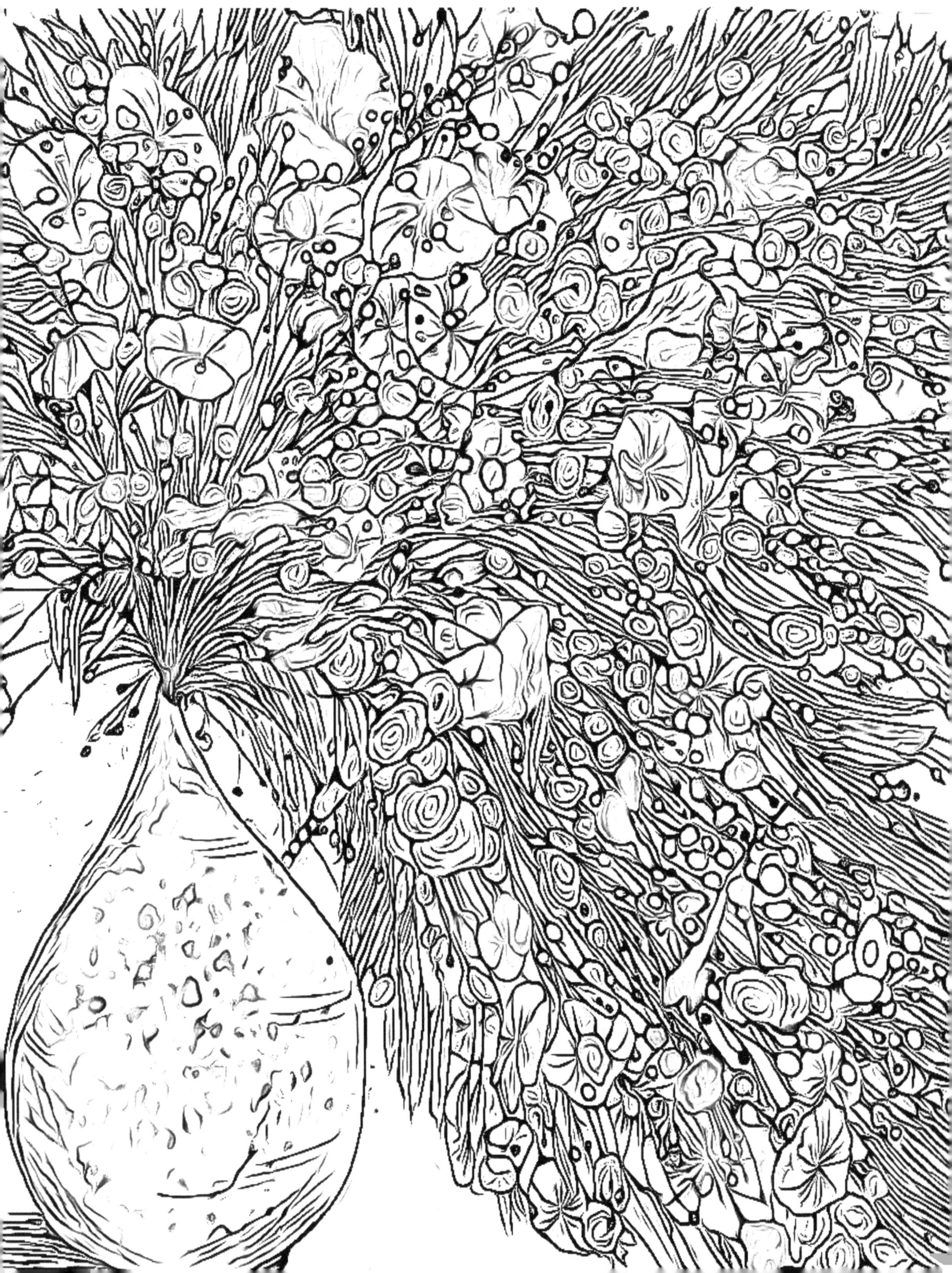

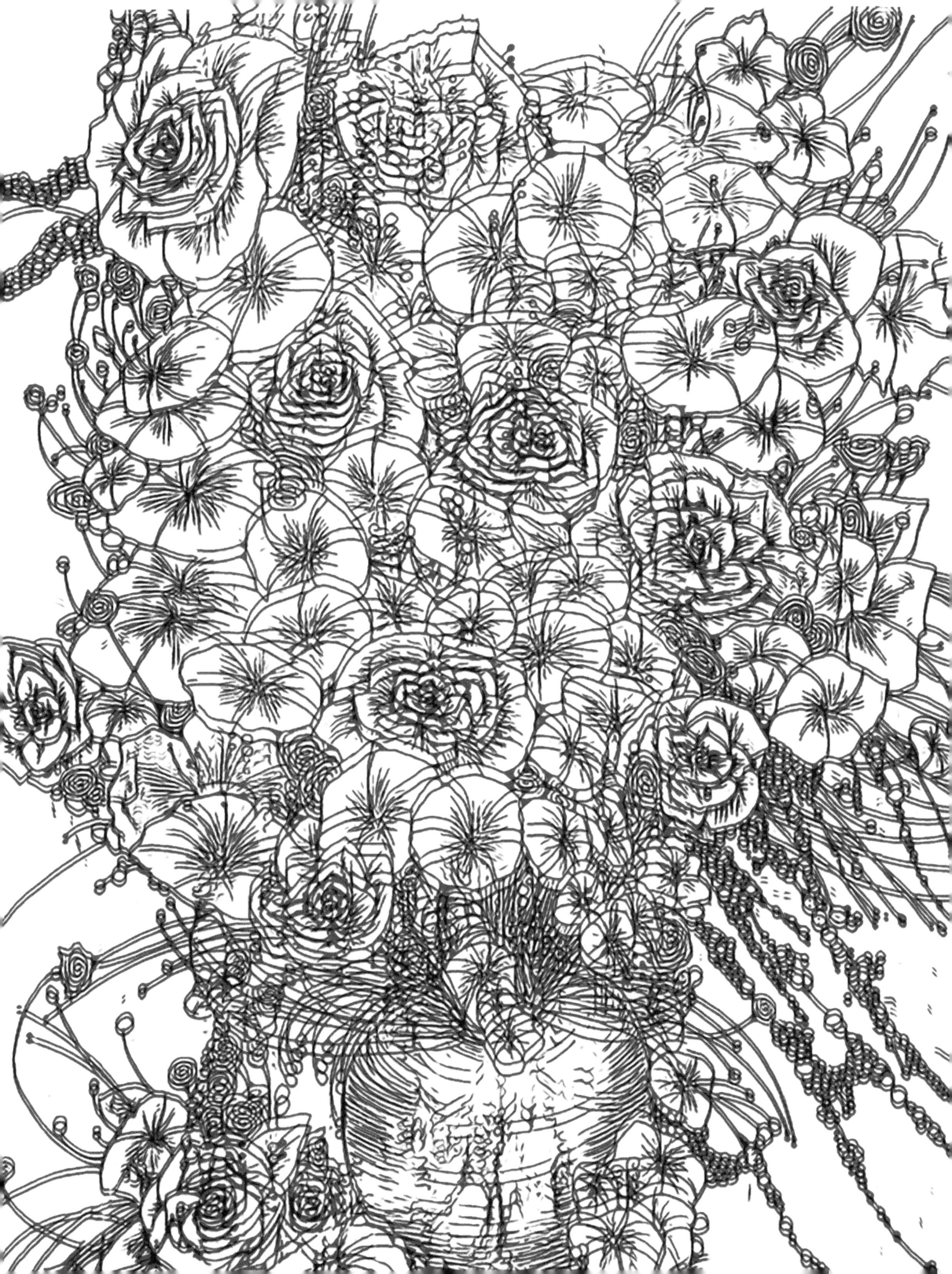

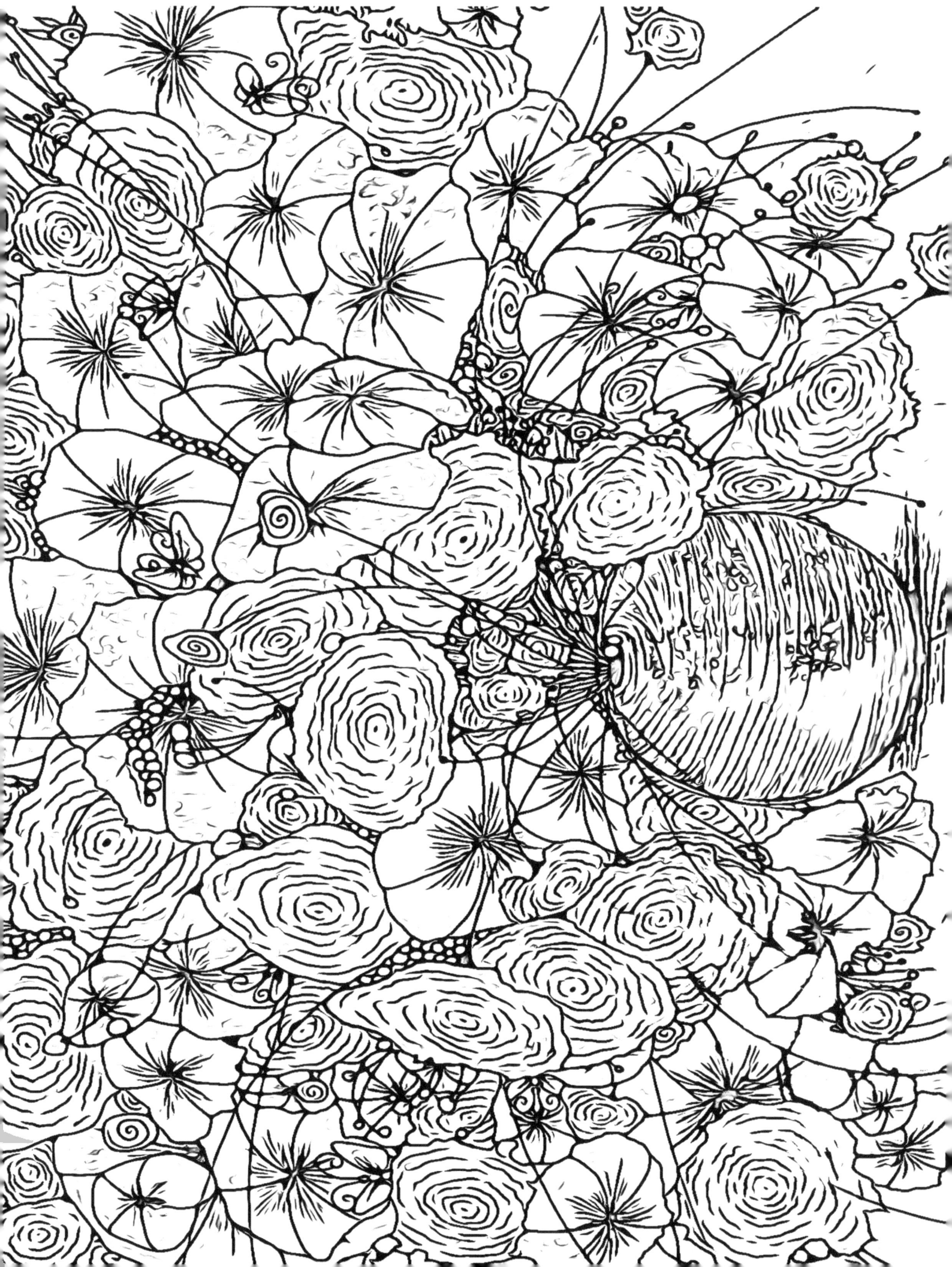

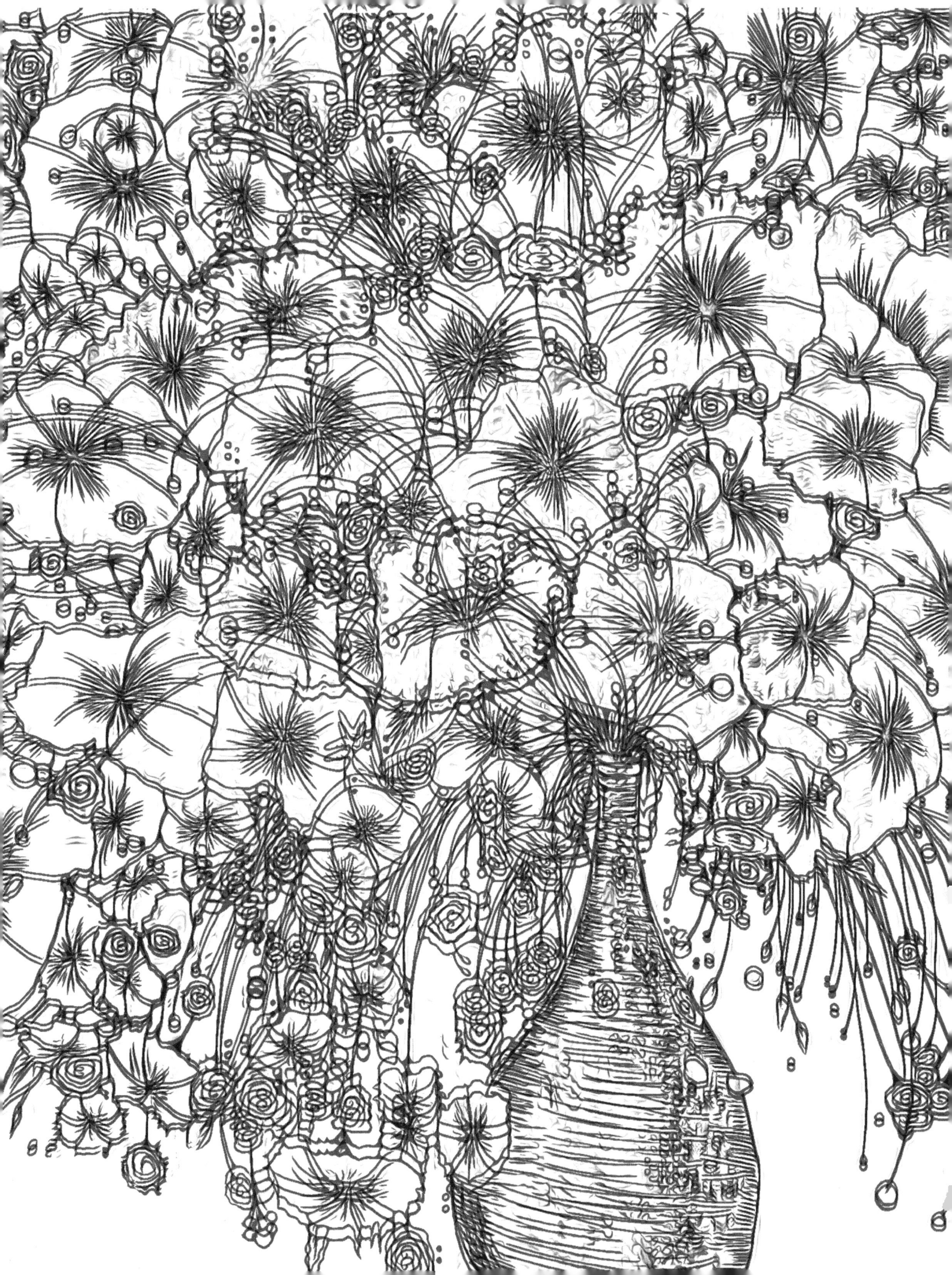

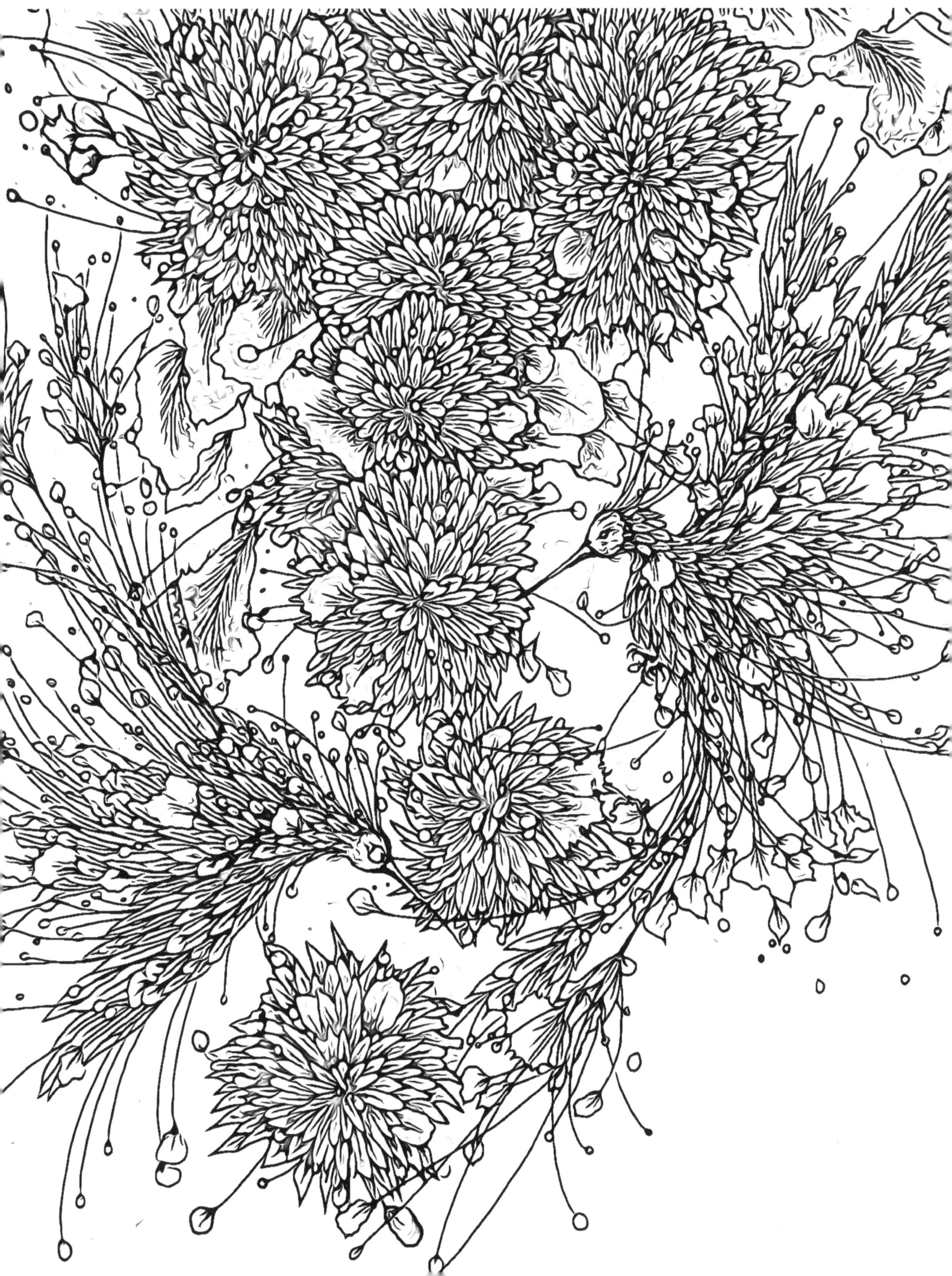

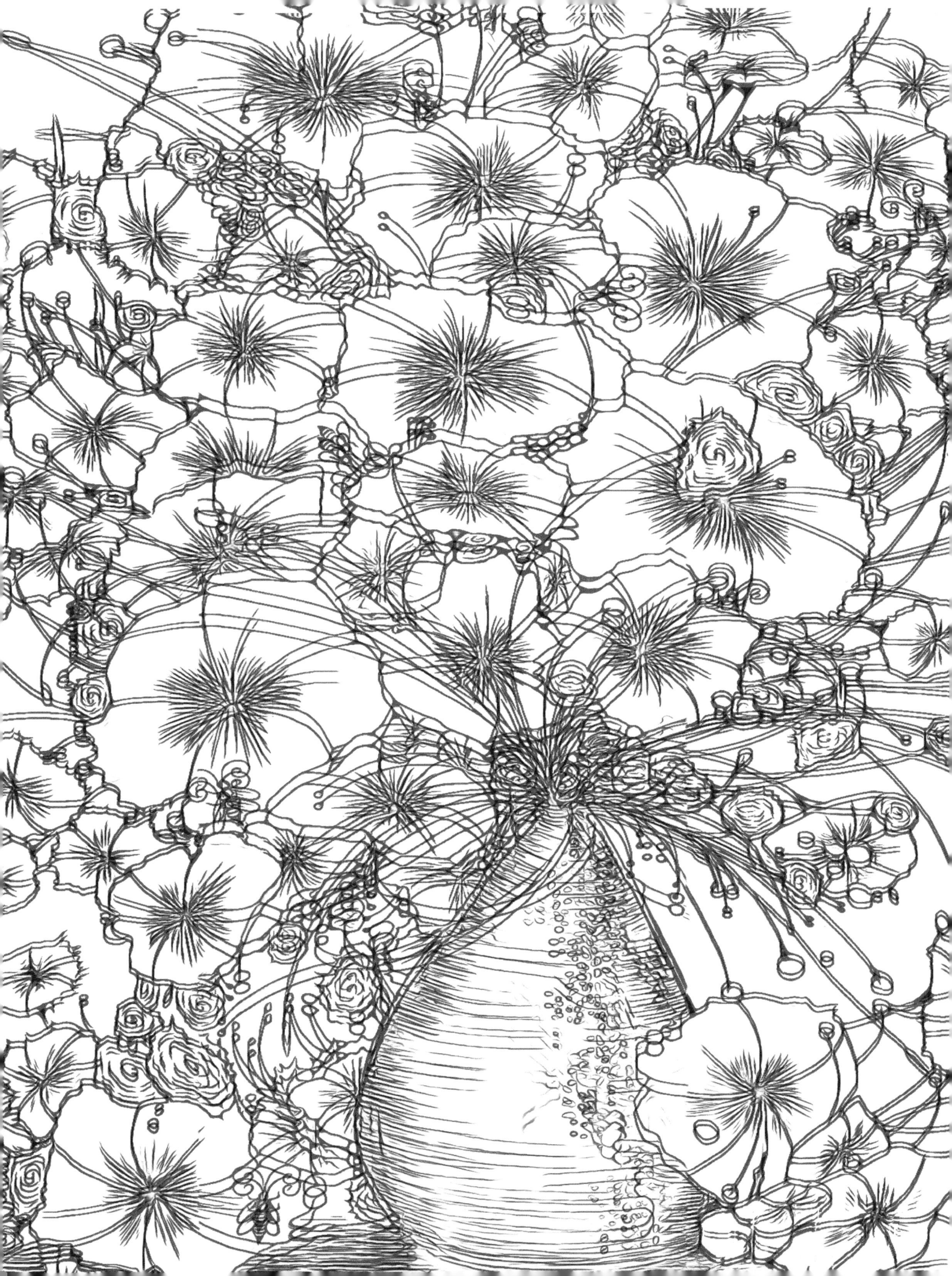

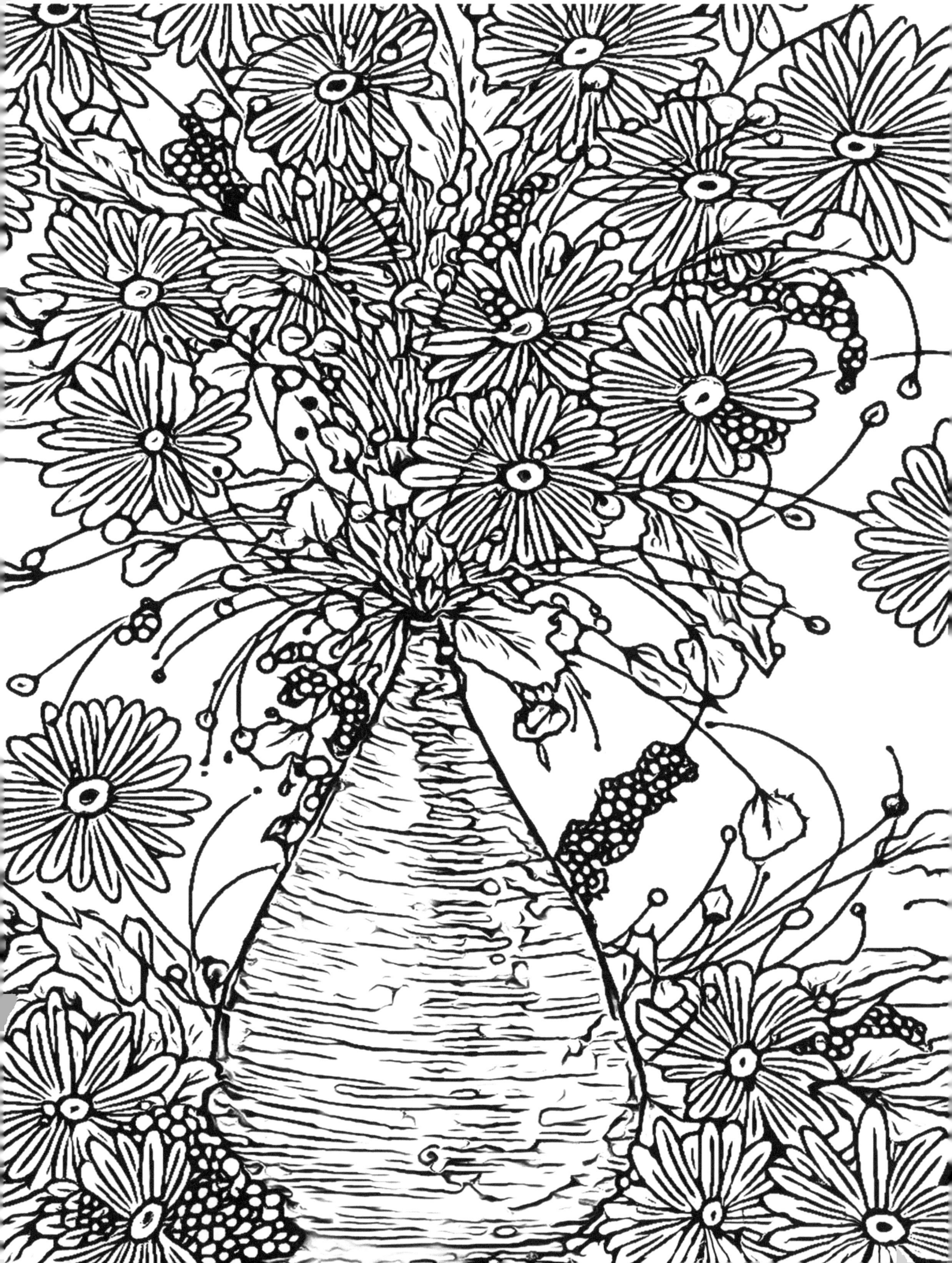

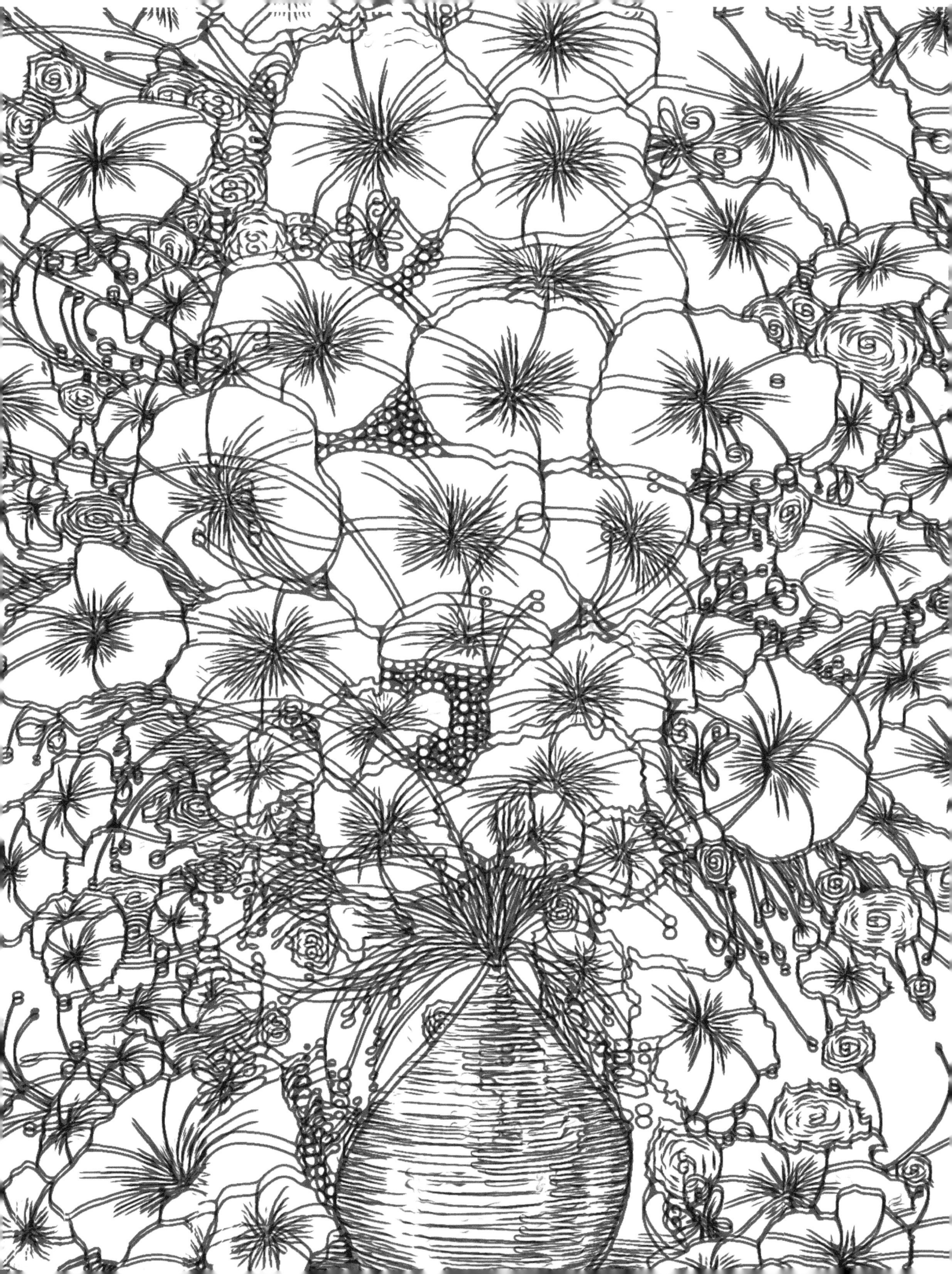

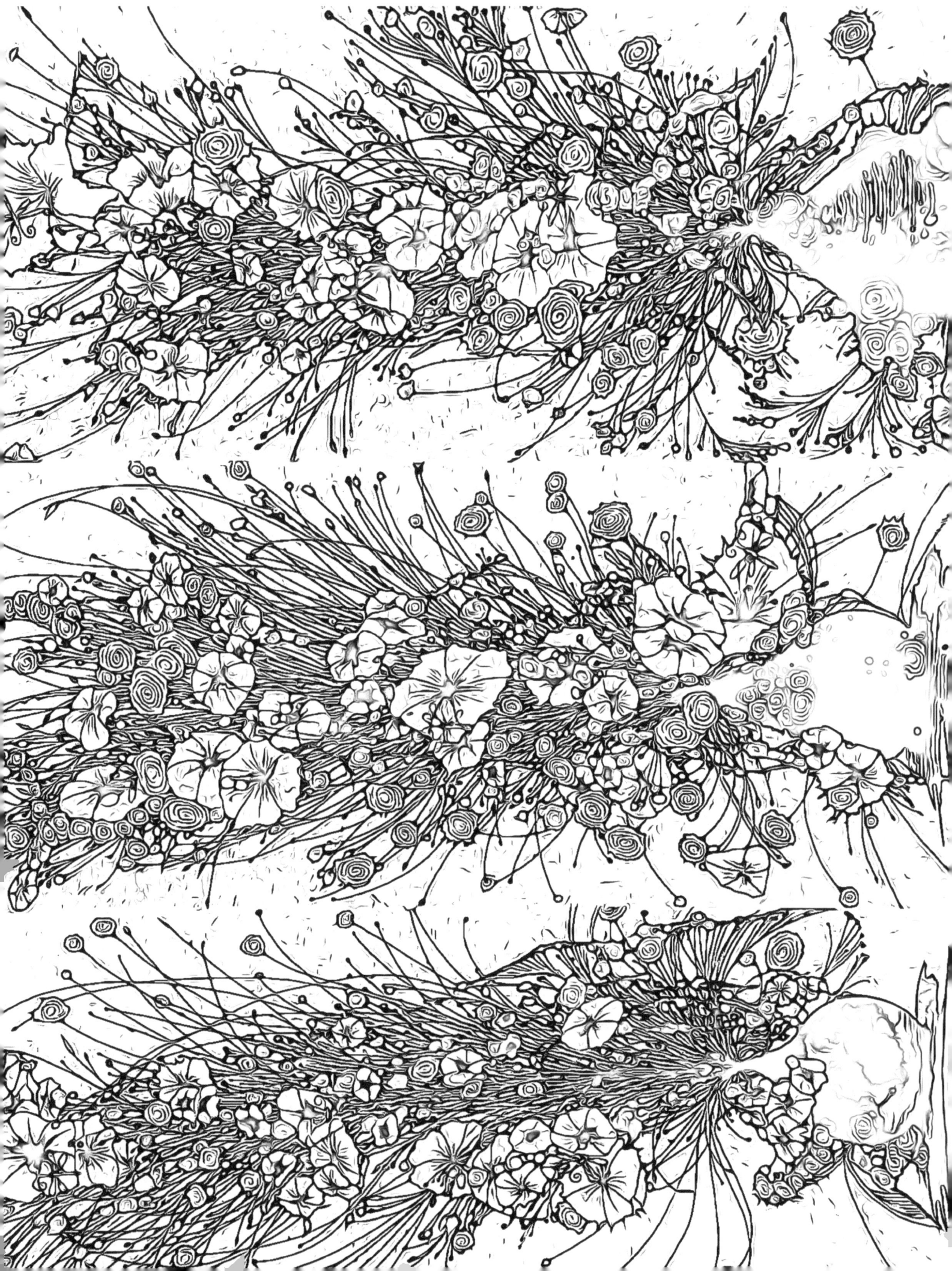

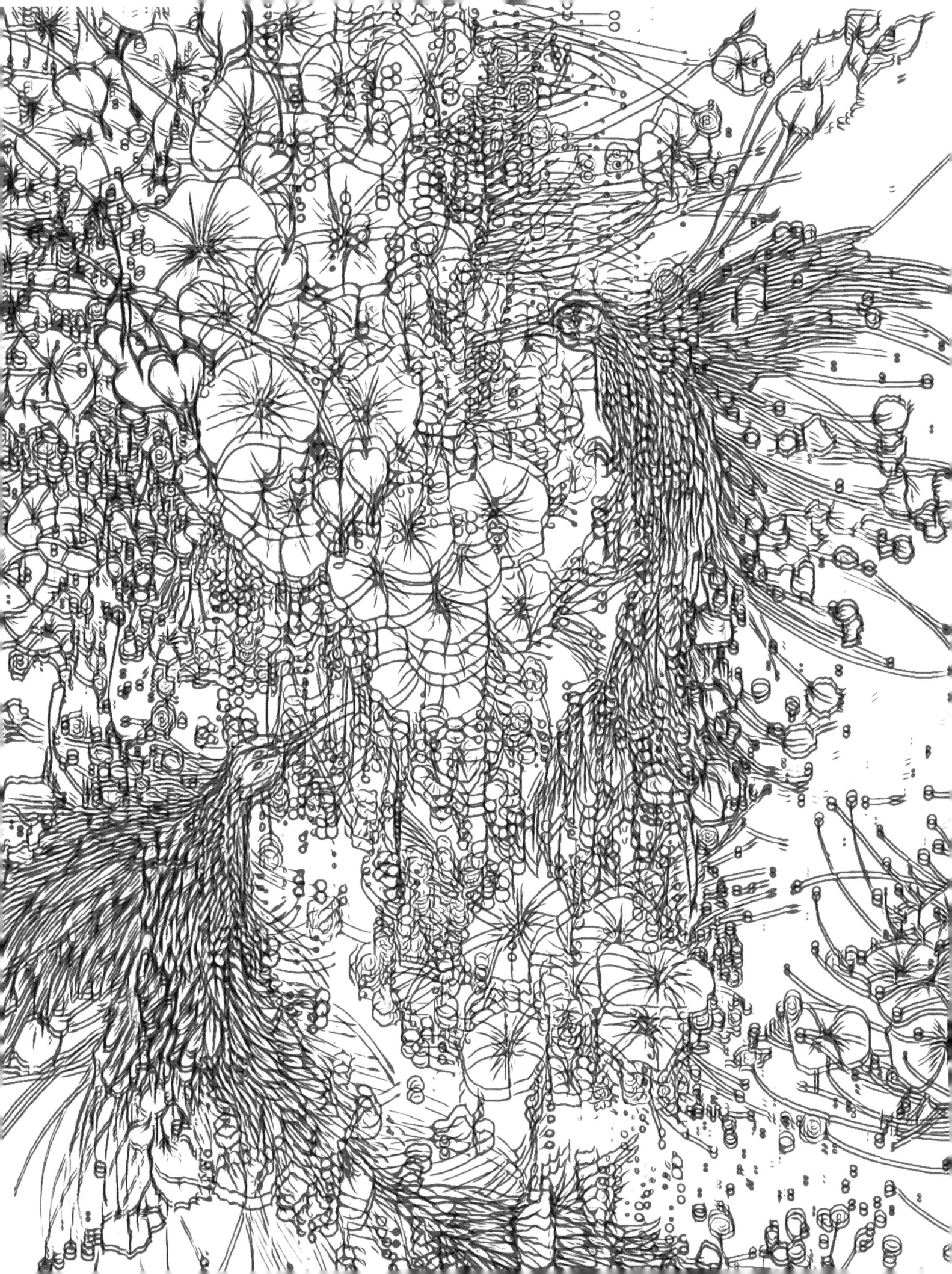

The End

Look for more coloring pages in Vibrant Creations Book II: Phoenixes

www.ingramcontent.com/pod-product-compliance
Lightning Source LLC
Chambersburg PA
CBHW051930210526
45473CB00006B/2196